First published in March 2015

The right of Ian Boddison to be identified as author of this book has been asserted in accordance with Sections 77 & 78 of the Copyright, Designs and Patents Act 1988

www.magic3weeks.co.uk

ISBN-10: 1501072072
ISBN-13: 978-1501072079

Cover design by Picked Jo
www.pickledjo.dunked.com
@pickledjo

The Magic of 3 Weeks

Ian Boddison

www.magic3weeks.co.uk

Contents

Foreword by Tom 'Big Al' Schreiter
International speaker and
Network Marketing Guru

Preface

1.	Magic of 3 Weeks	1
2.	Know What You Want	8
3.	Breaking The Goals Down	21
4.	Weekend of Planning	26
5.	Using a ToDo List	33
6.	The Daily Routine	42
7.	Putting it all together	50
8.	Fitting the magic into the day	60
9.	Keeping goals in focus	64
10.	Is it worth it?	79
	Epilogue	83

Foreword

Will power? That's overrated.

Ian has it right. Daily routines and habits ... over time ... will make our goals come true.

Will power is too much effort, especially if we are tired.

Habits and routines? Well, we just do habits and routines without even thinking about it.

Ian has been on a powerful journey of personal development for many years and has a reputation for setting goals and tracking those goals in a way that really works.

So this book is for anyone who wants more out of life because it shows how to form positive habits that can transform your life.

I like practical guides, I don't like theory, excessive planning and other time consuming efforts. In other words, I want results.

Enjoy Ian's system of habits and routines that make goal achieving possible.

Tom "Big Al" Schreiter
http://www.BigAlBooks.com

Preface

Everyone is looking for success!

Success for everyone means a different thing. For some it is financial, for others it is contribution and for many it is about family. But for everyone success needs defining before it can be obtained.

Here you will find all the help you need to decide what constitutes success for you. Then once you know what success is, how to form the habits that can make that success a reality.

This book is itself testament to the ideas and processes which it contains. For years the author has thought about writing a book but for most of that time never took any steps to make that happen.

Using the techniques explained here, that thought became a goal. Once it was a goal, habits were formed which took the idea and made it reality through systematic daily steps. And here it is, the result of that process, the finished book.

It may or may not be a book that you wish to write. It could be virtually anything that you want to achieve, anything you want that meets your definition of success. In the following pages you will find all the information you need to work out what it is you want and then to go after that using simple daily habits.

This information is not limited to just getting what you want. It is also about the journey through life. It will help you enjoy daily life more. Just having a direction will bring about more happiness. Plus here you will find numerous insights into moving towards the good life.

Learning to set goals and develop positive habits has changed my life. It doesn't happen overnight; it is a process that never really ends. It is my wish that the ideas contained here are helpful to you and that you are able to take some of them and apply them. It is my wish that they will help you on your journey towards the good life.

The Magic of 3 Weeks

Chapter 1

Magic of 3 Weeks

For a number of years I have been using, developing and continually refining the techniques that I am to share with you in the following pages. It is my sincere hope that they prove as useful to you as they continue to be for me.

What is so special about 3 weeks you may well ask?

Initially this was an arbitrary time frame which just happened to be adopted because a table covering a three week period fitted nicely onto an A4 sheet of paper. Making a table that fitted onto a single sheet and finding that table worked best if it covered three weeks. That is how it all started! However this somewhat accidental time period was reinforced as being useful when it was read that psychiatrists generally agree that it takes human beings 21 days of repetition to create a habit regardless of whether that habit is good or bad, constructive or destructive. Naturally the subject of this book is the forming of good, constructive habits. Although what is a good habit for one person may be inappropriate for another person by virtue of all people having different needs, different desires and different goals.

As well as making practical and convenient use of a single sheet of paper and fitting in with an accepted principle of how human beings form new habits, the transition from one period of three weeks to the next has also proved an ideal interval to review the previous period and to plan for the next. Every third weekend provides perfectly for this opportunity. During this natural interlude one can look at what worked well during the previous session and make appropriate changes for the following three weeks based upon both experience and ever evolving life situations and short term goals. As mentioned above, the techniques described here have been continually developed and refined over an extended timescale and, if they are to work effectively, they need to continue this evolution through changes made from one three week period to the next.

The use of a single sheet of A4 paper has already been mentioned. In this digital age some readers will immediately be thinking of ways to use a spreadsheet, website or other virtual means to replace the paper. However, please resist this urge. There is something special about the physical process of ticking off a task when it is completed; something that cannot be replicated with a digital alternative. The use of technology brings much to our lives and can replace much of what we used to do with paper but this is not one of those activities. Especially in an otherwise digital world, using paper for this purpose gives it an importance above and beyond many of the other activities of life.

There is no shortcut to forming habits. It always requires repetition regardless of whether the activity seems attractive or onerous at the time. Habits are learned most effectively when not too many are tackled at a time and using a repetition of three weeks means that important habits can be established first before moving onto other desirable behaviours. Just like when building a muscle in the body, consistent effort is required. It is of little use to rest all week and exercise on the last day; far better to undertake exercise every day. So it is with forming habits. Likewise, the greatest growth occurs when the activities that we undertake require great effort because we really do not feel in the frame of mind to be doing them. Just as muscle growth is greatest when we push our bodies to do just that little bit more exercise.

Most people, myself included, find that some activities that we want to undertake regularly never become established habits to the extent that they are performed instinctively and without prompting. Such tasks will doubtless remain included within our routine far beyond just one period of three weeks. Indeed there is no reason why some important tasks should not appear for months or even years, perhaps even after they have become established as firm habits. Having established an important habit, continued repetition and accountability ensure that this habit is not lost. Having a 'Daily Routine' is an effective way to make oneself accountable – self accountable.

The Daily Routine which follows should not be thought of in total isolation. Some mention of the use of a daily ToDo List will be made although this in itself could be the subject of another entire book. Indeed many books on the keeping and managing of ToDo Lists have already been written. Additionally goals and goal setting are another essential aspect of a successful and rewarding life. It is assumed that the reader already has at least some short term goals. Again, there are many excellent books on the subject of goal setting. Because goal setting is considered to be such an

5

integral part of a successful and meaningful life, an overview of the subject will be covered here. A simple, step by step guide will be presented instead of an in depth method. The intention is to allow the process to be started sufficiently. It is hoped that further reading will be sought on the subjects of setting goals and achieving goals.

Like all good things, the Daily Routine and with it the habits that are formed needs to evolve and develop. This is not a process that one completes once and then leaves aside. Instead through a process of action, review, modification and once again action the system becomes ever more useful. Each iteration brings improvement. But in the end the key word is 'action'.

> " Some things you have to do every day. Eating seven apples on a Saturday night instead of one a day just isn't going to get the job done. "
> **- Jim Rohn**

Throughout this book I have largely assumed that the reader works in some kind of employment for a number of hours during the week and has weekends free from work commitments. Obviously this is a sweeping generalisation as every individuals' time commitments are different. It is up to you to apply the ideas as you see fit and as they best align with your personal circumstances. I urge you to try, modify to suit your needs and improve upon the ideas in this book. But most of all have fun using the ideas to help sculpt your life into what you want it to be.

The Magic of 3 Weeks

Chapter 2

Know What You Want

If we don't know what we want it is very difficult to get it. Even if we do succeed in getting what we want, how will we know if we were unaware of what we wanted in the first place? Knowing what we want is the essence of setting goals.

Before embarking on any journey it is essential to have a good idea of the intended destination. If we plan a holiday trip, we would not turn up at the railway station and board the first train to arrive at the platform! Rather we would know where we intended to reach and plan the steps of the journey so that we arrive at the right place. Even if a train is cancelled we would not allow this setback to prevent us making our trip. We would find an alternative train, bus or taxi to complete that stage of the journey. It would be an inconvenience, it will probably delay our arrival and it will take us away from our original plans. But it won't prevent us completing the journey.

And so it should be with our journey through life.

First we need to have a clear idea of what we want to achieve, the destination at which we intend to arrive. Only then can we understand the stages of the journey that must be completed to ensure that we reach our destination and get the results that we desire. These things that we desire are our goals. They may change over time but if we don't start with some goals in place then we have no chance of ever achieving them.

As children we were adept at knowing exactly what we wanted. There were endless toys that we wanted to have, places we wanted to go, sweets we wanted to eat and games we wanted to play.

As adults we need to relearn the ability to dream and then to turn those dreams into solid goals. There are many excellent books about goal setting but here is a simple 5 step process to get you started. It is important that you take the time to do this across two consecutive days such as a weekend because as you sleep between the days your subconscious mind will work on the list you create on day one. It is important not to underestimate the power of the subconscious mind. That is where our real power lays and using simple techniques to harness that hidden power can increase one's progress immensely.

> " Goals are the fuel in the furnace of achievement. "
> **- Brian Tracy**

Step 1 – Empty your mind

On day one set aside about an hour. Get yourself a blank sheet of paper and start to jot down things you would like. Don't allow yourself to place limits on what you come up with by saying "I can't afford it" or things like "I would never be able to do that". The only limits are that it must be possible. So don't include being able to turn invisible or being able to visit the surface of the sun!

If you have never done this kind of exercise before then you should aim for a list of at least 20 goals. More would be better and an experienced goal setter should be able to list 50 or more goals quite readily. Try using this list to help with ideas:

- Where would you like to live?
- Where would you like to eat?
- What places would you like to see?
- What languages would you like to learn?
- What would you like to experience?
- What car(s) would you like to drive?
- What skills would you like to learn?
- Which charities and good causes would you like to be able to help?
- What bank balance would you like to have?
- When would you like to retire?

The items on the list do not have to be great long descriptions. Just a short note that makes sense to you is sufficient for now. So for example if you want to visit Istanbul and learn about some important mosques and other historic sites then just write down 'Visit Istanbul' or even simply 'Istanbul'.

Never be tempted to believe that these goals do not need to be written down. Goal setting cannot be done in one's head because until a goal is written down it is only a wish. Our minds simply are not good at processing long lists unless those lists are written down. Whenever anything is written down it is taken out of the mind and it is in the space between the mind and the paper where solutions come into being; where the magic happens.

The simple process of committing goals to paper has an amazing power. In fact until it is written down it is no more than a wish. Once processed through pen and paper it takes on its own form and emerges fully a goal. The importance of writing goals down cannot be stated strongly enough.

Step 2 – Guess how long

Once your list is complete and has at least 20 things on it, go through the list and write next to each item one of these numbers: 1, 3, 5, 10. These represent the approximate number of years that you think it will take you to achieve that goal. They are only vague timescales. If you think it will take less than a year still put down 1; if you think perhaps more than 10 years is required then still use 10. Your list should have an approximately equal split between all the time scales and a lack of either 1's or of 10's indicates that you need to think a bit more deeply about the things that you want. However, if this is your first time completing this exercise, don't worry too much about the spread of the numbers. The more times that you make a list of your goals, the more you should be aware of trying to get a more equal distribution of times but also the more that distribution will come naturally as goals come to mind with greater ease.

At the very start of your goal setting journey when you are new to the process, you may want to try writing out a list every few days until it comes more naturally and flows more easily.

Step 3 – Give it to your subconscious mind

Now put the list away and forget it! It is easy to think that this step is unnecessary, but trust me here; this is one of the most important parts of the process of goal setting. This is where the enormous hidden power of your mind gets harnessed and without you even realising it is happening.

Get on with your day and don't try to consciously think about the list, if it comes into your mind that fine but don't dwell on it. However, if you do remember it shortly before bedtime then get it out and read through it once then put it away again. If you can read it out loud then so much the better. This will help your subconscious mind to start processing the list while you are asleep which is where the magic of goal setting really happens.

> " Whatever we plant in our subconscious mind and nourish with repetition and emotion will one day become reality. "
> **- Earl Nightingale**

When it is not concentrating on a subject and especially during sleep the human mind has an incredible ability to come up with fantastic solutions to problems. Like the muscles of the body the mind needs regular exercise to keep it at top form and the more often it is tasked with processing goals the better it will become. It is always best to write down the list one day from instinct then to allow the mind to process it during sleep. This way, when it is revisited the following day it will be with a new level of insight that is more aligned to what one actually wants from life.

Step 4 – Find what matters

On day two it is important that you do not look at the list you made the previous day. Not even a little peek! Now is the time to find out which of the things that are listed are the ones that really matter to you. Again set aside about an hour, get yourself a blank sheet of paper and start to jot down a list of your goals just as you did previously. It is essential that you do not refer to your previous list because the goals you write down the second time will be the ones that really matter. The ones that you have forgotten are not that important.

You might like then idea of them and they may seem attractive, but if you have forgotten them overnight then they are not really important to you. It is probable that overnight you have thought of more goals to add to the list and these should be added as they come to mind. Remember, this first part where the list is written out is a case of emptying the mind of ideas and capturing those ideas on paper. Just let the goals flow.

Once again, at the beginning you should aim to list a minimum of 20 goals and increase this number as you repeat the process again and again over time. Having made your list, just like the day before go through them and label them with either 1, 3, 5 or 10 for the number of years you think it will take you to realise that goal. Don't think too much about the numbers, simply jot down the number that seems right.

For free resources to help you get the most out of The Magic of 3 Weeks including a ready made goal setting sheet, see the website:

www.magic3weeks.co.uk/free

Step 5 – Identify the Vital Few

Now we are going to put aside the 5 year and the 10 year goals. They are still important but we are going to consider the shorter term goals first. The simple fact that you have taken time to think about and, most importantly, write down your goals will have a huge impact on you achieving them. Once the 5 and 10 year goals have been removed, if most of the original list still remains, then also eliminate the 3 year goals. However, if the 1 and 3 year goals are about half the original list then take them all onto the next step. It will depend on how balanced the list was as to whether the 1 and 3 year goals will be about half the full list or not. The aim here is simply to get the list down to a manageable size of goals that can be worked on immediately. About a dozen is perfect if you are starting off. As you become more experienced at setting goals you will naturally get a better feel for how many suits you best. The exact numbers are not important provided the list feels manageable to you.

From this list of either just 1 year goals or 1 and 3 year goals we are going to extract the Vital Few according to the Pareto Principle which is also known as the 80/20 rule. This principle says that things divide naturally into two groups: the Vital Few (20%) and the Trivial Many (80%). For example, in a business 20% of the customers will account for 80% of the sales and from your wardrobe you will wear 20% of your clothes 80% of the time! Just go and check you wardrobe and you will see it holds true.

When applied to your list of goals, if you were to complete all of them then just 20% of them would have contributed to 80% of the improvement you would have made in your life. Finding that Vital Few really is a skill that can only be learned through experience. The best way to learn this skill is by trying to work out which are the Vital Few and accepting that some of the time you will get it wrong! A word of warning, the Vital Few are seldom the quickest or easiest goals on your list.

For more information on Pareto's Vital Few as it is applied to goals, goal setting or tasks that you want to accomplish and methods for identifying them, I highly recommend Brian Tracy's excellent book: 'Eat That Frog'.

You should aim to have between 3 and 8 goals as the Vital Few. These will be the goals to work on until the next goal setting time which I suggest you plan for 3 months time so that you have quarterly goals to work towards. These quarterly goals should be written out and pinned up in a prominent place where you see them every day. Places like near the kettle and the inside of the wardrobe door are ideal.

If you get the feeling that the goals you have written out have not yet had the opportunity to evolve sufficiently or you simply require a bit more practice then feel free to again go through the exercise of writing out your goals, setting timescales for them all and identifying the Vital Few. The more you practice, the better you will get. However, do recognise that the list will never be perfect so do not be tempted to wait for an ideal list before moving on with the next section and taking action.

Having committed to a set of goals and taken action you can always choose not to wait for 3 months but instead review them again in 3 weeks rather than waiting for the next quarter. However, once you start on a 3 week Daily Routine, do not break part way through. If you find the goals you have set require revision then see the 3 weeks through and revise them at the end of that period.

As an aside, you might like to encourage your family members to set goals in a similar fashion and then compare the various family goals. Not only will the common goals naturally be important ones to work on first, but knowing the goals of your partner and children can enable you to help them achieve their goals. Achieving goals with others is always more satisfying than doing so alone. Plus there is immense satisfaction in using your new skills to help others who you care about.

The Magic of 3 Weeks

Chapter 3

Breaking Down The Goals

A journey between two cities will involve a number of different roads to travel along and on the way several towns, villages and places of interest will be passed through. Perhaps even other cities will be passed during the course of the journey. The further apart the starting location and the destination, the more roads that will need to be used and the more places that will be encountered during the journey. Parts of the journey will be on major roads where speeds are high and other parts will be much slower on minor roads. But all parts of the journey are just as important to reaching the final destination. It is not possible to miss out part of the journey and successfully reach the intended final destination.

It is exactly the same when it comes to the journey through life to reach the destination of a goal. Some goals will be close and involve a short journey utilising just a few 'roads' and passing through just a few intermediate places. Other journeys to goal achievement will require a much more complicated route involving learning new skills, making new contacts and reaching a number of places along the journey.

Just like a journey between two cities, you are certain that you will reach your chosen destination. You might find a road closed or you may well take a wrong turning. But you will find a way to get to the place where you want to end up. When you take a wrong turning you don't give up on ever getting to your destination, instead you think briefly about where you went wrong, you look at the map (or curse the SatNav!) and establish exactly where you are before planning a new route to your destination based on the new information you have about where you are now. That new route might involve retracing your steps back to where you made the deviation from the original route or it might involve cutting across country to rejoin the original planned route or possibly even finding a completely new route.

When we set off on a journey to an unfamiliar city it is usually not just the destination alone that matters. We also want to enjoy the trip. We look at the scenery, we enjoy the experiences of the towns and villages we pass through and at some we might stop at for a short look around. Even if we want to arrive as expediently as possible we will use the intermediate places (or maybe motorway junction numbers) as an indicator of our progress.

Again, it is exactly the same with the journey through life to reach a goal. Enjoying the journey, keeping track of progress and celebrating the intermediate steps will not just make the whole process of achieving the goal more enjoyable. It will also help to keep you on the right road, heading in the right direction and spotting wrong turnings early so as to minimise delays. A big goal can seem too far off and too difficult to attempt in one go. But by breaking it down into distinct stages it becomes much more manageable. If there is something to celebrate at the end of each stage then it becomes enjoyable all the way through as well, which does wonders to maintain motivation.

Celebrating success along the way is an essential part of goal accomplishment. If for example, the process of working on the goal has taken you away from your partner some of the time, then going out for a meal together when that goal or part of the goal is complete would be a good way to celebrate. It is important that you plan what you will do mark the achievement of each part of the goal before you start work on it. That way you, and those around you, will have a very specific event to look forward to and to maintain motivation when times get tough, which they inevitably will sometimes.

Because recognising and celebrating small successes as well as larger ones is such an integral part of the process, it is recommended that once a pattern of three week routines is established, an achievement record is started. This is simply a case of looking back over the previous three weeks and writing down a number of things that have been achieved over the period. These do not need to be large! Learning to recognise and celebrate small successes can have a huge impact on overall satisfaction of life as well as increasing the staying power during tough times.

It is surprising how few people ever stop to consider what they want to get out of life; what their destination in the journey of life should be. If you have now listed your goals, written them down and identified the Vital Few then you are already significantly ahead of most of the people alive today. Purely creating goals is an end in itself because through this simple action much has been done to focus the mind to look for the opportunities that will bring about what we have decided we want. But it is also just the start of an exciting journey of self discovery and personal growth. Written goals are the bedrock of our life, the foundations on which all future improvements are built.

The Magic of 3 Weeks

Chapter 4

Weekend of Planning

Now that we have our list of Quarterly Goals written down and identified, and we understand that nearly always they need to be broken down into discrete stages, it is time to set aside a weekend to plan exactly what we want to achieve during the next 3 weeks. This needs to be done one goal at a time. We also have to take into account all the other things in life that we have to do and want to get done.

Pick one of the shortlist of goals and start by writing down all the reasons why this goal is important. Consider what will be gained once this goal has been achieved. The positive feelings that it will provide and the pleasures it will bring. Also write down the problems that it will solve and the troubles and pain which will be avoided. People are motivated to gain pleasure and avoid pain. The latter is generally a stronger motivation and it is important that we understand exactly why we want to realise this specific goal. The motivation behind the goal is the single biggest factor that will determine success or failure in goal achievement. The scale, length and difficulty of the tasks that comprise the goal have far less impact on the final result than the level to which one is compelled to succeed in completing the tasks. It is essential therefore that lots and lots of reasons why we want to complete the goal are identified right at the start of the process. These allow us to refer back to them as a reminder when things get tough and other life distractions seem more pressing or attractive.

Having established a clear idea why we want to achieve the goal we must now write down all the things that need to be done in order to achieve the goal. This may be a new skill that has to be learned, which in itself will consist of finding a suitable book, course, DVD or person from where the skill can be learned. It could also be a task that has to be undertaken like painting a room or writing a report. Whatever the things are that need doing, write them all down paying particular attention to the ones that can be done straight away. Again, do not be tempted into believing that writing them down is unnecessary because we are unable to do this effectively in our heads. Writing down the ideas in our head gives space between us and the idea. It is in this space that the magic happens.

> " If you have a goal, write it down.
> If you do not write it down, you do not have a goal - you have a wish. "
> **- Steve Maraboli**

Once you have this list for all the goals on your shortlist it is time to create another list for the things you need or want to do every day for other areas of your life. For example, when I was on a course of medication I used to regularly forget to take it until I included 'Take medication' as a daily task.

In a future chapter we are going to create our first Daily Routine that we will be working with for the next 3 weeks. There an example at the end of this book and further examples are available online at www.magic3weeks.co.uk/free which you may want to look at to give you some idea of where we are heading. This might provide a better idea of the things that need including in the list of tasks for goal achievement and give some ideas for the sort of items that you might want to add to help with life in general.

You might also want to consider having a Weekly Routine. This is simply a task that is included on the Daily Routine which refers to a task or tasks which change depending on the day of the week. Examples of the sort of task that should appear on here is to water the houseplants or to put out the rubbish bins; both of which are reasonably essential tasks but probably don't want doing everyday! It is far from necessary to have a Weekly Routine especially at the beginning but you may find that once you have used a Daily Routine for some time you will probably want to add a Weekly Routine as well. There is also an example of a Weekly Routine on the website that accompanies this book: www.magic3weeks.co.uk

The Daily Routine you will end up with will be a single sheet of A4 paper with 3 weeks across it and the number of tasks you have identified down it. The actual process of putting together the Daily Routine is best carried out over two days like a weekend. Start by creating a draft, then leave the final version until the next day after you have had chance to sleep on it. In that time your subconscious mind will have made some revisions and changes. You should aim to have between 12 and 25 tasks on the Daily Routine. The more of your day is allocated to the tasks on it, the more tasks that will appear.

The tasks should be divided into at least three sections: a morning 'bookend', a daytime section and an evening 'bookend'. Depending on your lifestyle, daily commitments and what you wish to achieve, you may want to divide the daytime section into two, three or maybe four sections.

These bookends are an absolutely critical component of the Daily Routine as we shall see. Having morning and evening 'bookends' and also a body section are essential features of the structure of the Daily Routine.

Because we can never plan what our day will throw at us and because things inevitably happen that need our time and attention, these sections are really important. No matter how chaotic our day becomes, we can always control how we start the day and how we end it. These are the morning bookend and the evening bookend. There should not be too many tasks in either of these and they should be reserved for the really important things that we absolutely want to do every day no matter what. If the daytime section is divided up then one section would be for tasks we really want to get done and the other for tasks that we would like to get done. The important part is that we always do the tasks on the morning and evening bookend no matter what. The first daytime section we always do unless some emergency gets in the way and the second daytime section we do our best to do every day but don't worry excessively if we miss a day, but missing everyday of a week would be a cause for concern.

We need at accept that no matter how much time and thought we put into deciding upon the tasks to include, we will get it wrong! Sorry, but that is inevitable. However, once we start working through the Daily Routine it is important to continue with it for the full three week without meddling. The next planning weekend will come around soon enough and with it the opportunity to start a completely new Daily Routine for the next three weeks. Although the reality will be that the next one will be based very much upon the previous one with modifications made to improve upon what went before. These really do evolve a little at a time both in content and in order.

The Magic of 3 Weeks

Chapter 5

Using a ToDo List

Most people already make use of a daily ToDo List and as you are reading this book, I am going to assume that you do. If, like me, you write out your ToDo List the night before then this task will form part of your evening bookend. Likewise, I always write three things that I am grateful for into my journal each evening so bringing my journal up to date and recording these gratitudes is another task within my evening bookend. Focussing on things for which we are grateful by itself, improves the way we see the world and increases our satisfaction with life.

It is important that the length of a ToDo List is limited otherwise it simply gets longer and longer with some tasks that will never get completed. These tasks might have been usurped by others or are no longer required or just tasks that you really don't want to do.

> " One of the secrets of getting more done is to make a To Do List every day, keep it visible, and use it as a guide to action as you go through the day.". "
> **- Jean de La Fountaine**

Not only should the size of the list be limited but a mechanism has to also be provided which removes these unnecessary tasks. Having a system for removal is needed as more often than not there is no way to evaluate the tasks that simply will never get completed. Because there is a feeling that they 'should' be completed the urge is to allow them to remain on the list despite their only real purpose being to clutter the list and get in the way of other more productive tasks.

Using a standard reporters' notebook is an effective implementation of a ToDo List. These books are low cost, readily available, small enough to be carried around and typically have approximately 20 lines for recording the tasks. 20 tasks is an ideal maximum for a ToDo List as it is not too long that the important tasks get swamped by the less important ones but equally it is sufficient to allow some flexibility in what is undertaken.

Tasks that are planned for the next 4 to 7 days should be included on this daily working ToDo List. Longer term tasks being incorporated on a master ToDo List which will inevitably be significantly longer. As and when tasks are transferred from the master list to the daily list is a matter of personal choice and will depend on the routines of one's daily life such as work patterns, etc. However, it is recommended that at least every three weeks during the planning weekend some tasks are moved onto the daily list. Personally I transfer tasks virtually every day.

During the evening bookend the ToDo List from the day gets rewritten excluding any tasks that have either been completed or which are no longer relevant. Some may be removed from the daily list and added to the master list if they still need completing but are going to left for a while. Anything else that has arisen through the day can also be added to the list provided there is sufficient room on the single sheet of the reporters' notebook. Rewriting the day's list in order before adding anything new will ensure that the tasks listed at the top will be the ones that have been on there the longest. A new task always starts at the bottom of the list and over time moves up the list until it is completed, removed or it reaches the very top of the list. The top task, being the oldest, will be treated slightly differently.

Now that we have a ToDo List prepared the night before we can include in the morning bookend a time to go through the list and again apply the Pareto Principle or 80/20 rule to the tasks that are there. 20% of the 20 tasks on the list is just 4 tasks and these will form the Vital Few. These 4 tasks could also be called the Premium Tasks because, if they are completed they will create as much positive progress as all the remaining tasks added together. Identifying these Premium Tasks takes practice but it is unlikely that the quickest or easiest tasks on the list will be the ones that we are searching for; the ones which hold the real magic. The task at the top of the ToDo List automatically becomes a Premium Task by virtue of it having been on there the longest. The other three Premium Tasks are those selected using the Pareto Principle.

Naturally 'Premium Tasks' makes an ideal slot to include in the Daily Routine.

When identifying the Premium Tasks, long term importance should be considered above urgency. We all have a tendency to react to our world only taking action in response to the goings on that happen around us. However if we can identify the things that are important to us and concentrate our efforts on the tasks that bring us closer to what we consider important, then we will achieve much more in less time. Of course we will always need to react to the situations we encounter as we can never predict when we will need to deal with an ill child, an unexpected gift or severe weather to name just a few. We should plan to minimise our reactive behaviour and increase our long term activities although it is a fact of life that emergencies and other urgent situations will inevitably arise.

It is possible that during the process of selecting the Premium Tasks that the ones chosen are always picked out because they absolutely have to be completed immediately and cannot be left for another day. If this happens more often than not, then it is a sure sign that one's life is being ruled by outside forces and not by long term goals. It is a natural tendency to simply cast this off and put it down to the way life is. But life really does not need to be purely reactionary. Setting aside small chunks to time to regularly dream, set goals and to make plans for how those goals might be achieved will have a massive effect on getting life under control and being able to allocate time to long term desires rather than the short term needs of the world. There is an incredible and immediate sense of inner peace that comes from simply taking control of the direction of life from all those external forces that have plans different to yours.

If a large part of your life is filled with commitments that cannot reasonably be moved around such as work shift patterns or fixed time family commitments then you may like to consider dividing the ToDo List into two distinct sections: one for tasks that can be completed at any time of the day and one for those which require others to be available. These latter tasks could be seeing an accountant who only works during the day or making phone calls to arrange family activities. By dividing up the tasks it is possible to arrange to only do the ones that can be done at any time when others are unavailable like early in the morning. This makes more efficient use of time and therefore accelerates the route to getting the things that are wanted out of life.

> " The future depends on what we do in the present. "
> **- Mahatma Ghandi**

At the end of the day, as part of the evening bookend, again the ToDo List is rewritten omitting any tasks that have been completed or that are no longer appropriate. However, this time when the first task on the list which is the oldest, is added again it has '1' written after it. If it remains undone and gets added the following evening it gets '2' written after it and then '3' the following day. Then if the next evening it still remains then it needs removing from the list completely. The reality is that the task has been on the ToDo List for a considerable time in order for it to get to the top of the list and has also been a Premium Task for three consecutive days and still remains uncompleted. As this is the case it is probably never going to get completed. Leaving it on the ToDo List would only clog up the list and prevent tasks that are important from getting included and achieved.

Much as there may be a feeling that a task 'should' be done, sometimes the reality is that it will never get done and we need to have a means of removing these tasks from the list before they block it up and prevent its usability. Removing tasks that have been on the list so long that they make it to the top and then don't get completed despite being a Premium Task for three consecutive days is a good way to ensure that all tasks have sufficient opportunity to be completed without allowing them to jeopardise the effectiveness of the ToDo List by clogging it up and bringing it to a grinding halt.

Should you consider a task that is about to be removed from the top of the list really important then it can be added to the end of the list and treated as a new task. If it were to remain at the top of the list it would only serve to prevent progress and eventually the ToDo List will become swamped with tasks that really 'should' be done but which are unlikely ever to get completed. The purpose of the ToDo List is to add to your future, not to distract from it and tasks that are not moving life forwards add nothing to the future. This can prove difficult at first as we all have tasks that we feel we 'must' carry out and removing one of these tasks from the ToDo List without first completing it can leave us feeling uncomfortable. Having a somewhat mechanical rule for removing the task at the top of the list after it has remained uncompleted for three days takes this out of our hands, but only if we follow the rule without deviation.

The Magic of 3 Weeks

Chapter 6

The Daily Routine

By this point you should have drafted your initial Daily Routine on the first day of the weekend. This will have been based upon the example at the end of this book and the template and examples available online at www.magic3weeks.co.uk/free. You should have let your subconscious mind work on it overnight and then revised it on the second day of the weekend. Accepting that it will never be perfect you now need to print it on a single sheet of A4 paper. If it won't fit on a single sheet of paper then you know for certain that you are attempting to fit too many tasks into your day.

On Monday morning when you first start your day you can look at the top of the list and complete the first task and tick it off with a line through the box. Then move onto the second, third and so on. There is something special that happens when you physically tick off the tasks listed on your paper sheet. It provides a feeling of accomplishment and also provides the motivation to carry on with the next task so that can be crossed off also. The boxes that are ticked off are deliberately small. This means that there is no room for an excuse! The simple fact is that all that matters is whether the task gets completed or not, why it gets completed or gets left is irrelevant. Everyone has days taken up by attending a conference, spending time with loved ones or simply enjoying a hobby. Such activities are essential to a balanced life. When the time comes to review the Daily Routine seeing lots of unticked boxes will be a sign that things are getting in the way a bit too much whereas if there are consistently no breaks then you will have to ask yourself if you are working a bit too hard at the expense of other life areas.

Having a morning bookend means that you will do your best to push yourself to accomplish the tasks within the bookend as you know that they are important to the overall progress of your life. You know that each day taken in isolation appears insignificant, but that through consistency these small tasks result in big changes over time.

This book is a real life example of this consistency. I had been writing this book for over two years and got little further than drafting the titles of the chapters. Then I added 'writing' as a 15 minute task to my morning bookend and within two months the manuscript was ready for proof reading. If that task had been allocated too much time then no doubt I would look at it and not start it because the thought of an hour sat at a keyboard was not appealing. 15 minutes seems much more bearable. The reality is that many days I would work well past the allotted 15 minutes but virtually every day I did a small amount. Furthermore, had the task been later in the day instead of being within the morning bookend I would have regularly put it off until later, a later that would never come! I know this because it had been included as a later slot on my Daily Routine on numerous occasions.

As previously noted, the Daily Routine will evolve over time. Each one will build upon the previous version and will change as the needs of your life evolve and grow but also as a result of what has been learned during the last three weeks. When you find that something that is important to you is not receiving the consistent time it requires then consider moving it to either the morning or evening bookend. However, it is important that only the absolute essential tasks reside here as only in truly exceptional circumstances should we allow them to remain uncompleted.

> " Consistency for me is everything. "
> **- Alexei Navalny**

The Daily Routine

Having completed the morning bookend we are ready to face the day contently knowing that no matter what happens, the most essential work to ensure our future has already been completed. This is why the goals that we explored in Chapter 2 are so vital. Without knowing what is truly important, we cannot decide which tasks we must complete to ensure our future and which ones we just do for present benefits or, perhaps we just do them out of habit when they contribute very little to our goals and to our future.

During our day we shall try to accomplish as many as possible of the tasks that comprise the main body of the Daily Routine. If we have split this into several sections then priority should be given to the first section first for exactly the same reasons as we discussed about getting the important tasks of the morning bookend completed so we know they are done before the events of the day get in the way. There will be some tasks that we have included that rarely, if ever, get completed. This is not a problem because every three weeks we will review the routine and eliminate, move up the sheet or revise these tasks.

At the end of the day during the course of the evening, make some time to complete the tasks that comprise the evening bookend. You may find it convenient to undertake these when you arrive home from work or you may need to set an alarm on your mobile phone to remind you to stop working and to get your evening bookend tasks completed. These tasks, like those of the morning bookend, should be kept to a minimum and should also be short tasks that either review the day which has just passed or else prepare for the following day. As previously mentioned, I jot down three things for which I am grateful each evening and this appears on my Daily Routine as 'Update journal and record gratitudes'.

If you use a daily ToDo List, now is also the time to write out the tasks that you intend to accomplish the following day. If you do not already use a daily ToDo List then I would strongly encourage you to start. The process of simply writing down what you want to achieve makes the accomplishment far more likely. Writing out the list of tasks the night before means that during sleep the subconscious mind will work on solutions to the problems that have already been identified for the following day. It will often come up with new and innovative ideas that will make the tasks easier.

There should not be too much more contained within the evening routine as it really should be a time to briefly review the day that has past and to prepare for the coming day. However, a couple of examples of other tasks I have included at times may serve to illustrate further. When I was travelling greatly in a previous job I would often skip meals which had an adverse effect on my moods so I included 'Eat a proper meal' within my evening bookend. This meant that I could quickly track how many days I missed out on a proper meal and make sure that at the very worst I didn't go more than a couple of days without a balanced diet. Similarly, I was on regular medication and frequently forgot to take it! But adding 'Take medication' to my evening bookend ensured that I didn't again skip a day due to my forgetfulness.

> " We forget that every good that is worth possessing must be paid for in strokes of daily effort. We postpone and postpone until those smiling possibilities are dead. "
> **- William James**

It's essential that once the Daily Routine has started, that it is completed by letting the three weeks run their course. It has to accepted that it will never be perfect. The challenge is to improve upon the previous Daily Routine each time that it is reviewed and revised. But make sure that the full three weeks are completed unchanged as this is where the magic happens. Note down ideas for what tasks would benefit from consolidating two or more into one, eliminating completely and which new tasks might need adding. These ideas will be invaluable during the next Planning Weekend, but do not be tempted to implement them until the next Daily Routine is created. Resist the urge to tamper with the Daily Routine part way through, it won't take long before the next Planning Weekend comes around and the routine can be properly revised.

The Magic of 3 Weeks

Chapter 7

Putting It All Together

Up to now we have looked at how we decide what we want through the use of elementary goal setting. We have identified which goals we shall concentrate our efforts upon and broken them down into manageable steps. We have then created a task list to help ensure we have an excellent chance of achieving our goals and finally we have created a Daily Routine with morning and evening bookends of tasks that we absolutely must do at the start and end of each day respectively. On our Daily Routine we also have one or more body section that we will seriously attempt to accomplish every day.

So let us review the whole process and see how it all fits together.

Every three months, set aside a break from the usual routine. If possible, physically go away on a break but if work and other commitments do not allow then just lighten the daily load as much as practically possible. Two weeks around the turn of the year, a week in March, two weeks in June or July and a further week in September are ideal times for these quarterly reviews. Not only are they approximately three months apart but they also align nicely with the natural seasons. Firstly around the time of Christmas and New Year, then again in the spring, this is an ideal time for planning outdoor activities for the summer months. Next is during the summer when most people want to take a break anyway so what better time to review one's goals and life direction. Then finally in the autumn, allowing for a review of the summer months and preparation for the dark evenings of winter which can be ideal for working inside on interesting projects. These times apply to the UK; they may not align so well with the seasons and yearly cycle in other parts of the world so some simple modification around this theme might be necessary.

It is during these quarterly breaks that the major life goals will be written out from memory. The very process of writing out goals from memory starts a magical process. It is surprising how much the list will change each time the process is carried out. But it is also surprising how many goals will remain constant and it is these which are the very important goals, the ones that really are strong desires and not just wishes or dreams.

> " Unless commitment is made, there are only promises and hopes...but no plans. "
> **- Peter F. Druker**

Whilst the process of writing out the goals does not take an enormous amount of time it is essential that some time is allocated to doing so. It cannot be rushed or fitted in between other things as it needs a clear, uninterrupted mind for it to be truly effective.

This list of goals is then refined so focus can be given to just a few at a time. The refined list will form the road map to use during the following three months to ensure arrival at the next stop on the journey through life. Each goal will be broken down into smaller steps and this, along with the various other things that need completing every day for work, family and other life commitments will form the basis of the all important Daily Routine which will serve for the next three weeks. After this time period the routine will be reviewed for what worked well and what was less successful, then a new version created for the next three weeks and so on for the entire three months.

> " When obstacles arise, you change your direction to reach your goal, you do not change your decision to get there. "
> **- Zig Ziglar**

Of course it is highly possible and desirable that one or more of the stated goals will get completed during the 3 month period and before the time comes to next review the goals. When any goal, no matter how minor, is completed this is cause for celebration. Every goal completion must be celebrated! The exact nature of the celebrations can be set at the same time as the goal getting task plan is formulated. Acknowledging the progress inherent in achieving a goal provides drive and motivation to move forward with vigour. As well as the act of celebrating this completion, the achievement should be written down on a separate list of successes. This list with provide great strength in future when sticking to the disciplines of the Daily Routine becomes taxing as at times it no doubt will. Looking back over the list will provide tangible evidence of the value of these daily disciplines and of the positive magic they create.

Once a goal is completed it should not be replaced with another until the time comes in the cycle to again review all the goals and set new ones. Instead the time allocated to the now completed goal can be used to push ahead with progress towards the remaining goals. This is a distinct benefit of always working on several goals at the same time. At the next 3 month goal setting stage a full complement of goals will again appear but do not be tempted to work on a new goal until this time comes around.

At the end of the quarter of a year (three months) it will be time to again review the list of life goals from memory and set more goals as the destination for the following three months. If possible, this process will be carried out during time off work and away from other life distractions. Where getting away is not practical, then setting aside two days (perhaps a weekend) is an adequate alternative. In any case, the effectiveness of the goal planning process will directly reflect the importance and priority that is given to it. Trying to cram it into the corners of the day will result in a rushed and inferior result. Having said that, rushed goal setting is much better than no goal setting and will instantly propel one ahead of others, most of whom have never even considered setting regular life goals.

Whilst working daily through the Daily Routine it is best to start at the top and work through to the bottom. However, this order should not be stuck to so rigidly when it doesn't make sense to do so or when a task cannot be completed at that time.

Sometimes a task must remain incomplete that day and others further down the routine should not be neglected. If no progress is being made on a particular day and the whole process seems too much of a chore, remember that any task completed is better than no task completed. In these cases just having a daily list of tasks can lead to something being achieved however small.

> If no progress is being made on a particular day and the whole process seems too much of a chore, remember that any task completed is better than no task completed

It is also important, regardless of the rest of the routine, to complete the tasks that comprise the evening bookend at the end of the day. Once the end of the day arrives, forget the body of Daily Routine for that day and complete the evening bookend before relaxing knowing that the day has been one of progress towards the stated goals. Never end the day thinking about what didn't get done. Always celebrate what has been achieved even if this is only the morning and evening bookends. Because these are important tasks for goal achievement, completing just these ensures that the day has resulted in positive progress and that is to be celebrated.

Some people find it difficult to remember to complete the evening bookend. They get so engrossed in their evening that the bookend gets left until they are ready to retire for the night by which time it is too late. In such cases, setting an alarm on one's watch or mobile phone can be helpful to point out when it is time to stop working for that day and to start the tasks of the evening bookend. Sometimes this will take a large dose of self discipline and the rewards will be far from obvious. However, by consistently pushing oneself to complete the tasks, positive habits are formed that ensure future success.

Whenever the temptation to neglect completing the tasks presents itself, it is worth remembering that each time that temptation is overcome, the habit of successful behaviour is reinforced. This is especially true of the morning and evening bookends. Completing the tasks of the bookends create the tracks which will guide our lives to the destination established with our goals. The tasks which form the body of the Daily Routine keep our lives firmly on these tracks and moving forward with deliberate intent.

It is highly likely that some tasks on the Daily Routine will be completed rarely, if at all. Unsurprisingly these will be the tasks that will need reviewing first when it is time to create a new Daily Routine for the next three weeks. But remember to stick with the routine that has been created for the entire three weeks even if appears that it is not working. It is through sticking with the routine that the magic happens. Soon the three weeks will have passed and a new revised version will be created incorporating all that has been learnt from staying with the routine to completion. Very often, when a task regularly remains uncompleted it is not the task that is wrong but it is the position that is wrong. Simply moving it up or down the Daily Routine will ensure that it get more attention. However, be careful to ensure that tasks included on the routine really have to be completed. On occasions a task regularly remaining uncompleted actually happens because the subconscious mind understands that it just doesn't need doing. Despite it logically appearing very desirable, some tasks just do not need to be carried out regularly and the human mind is very good at identifying these unless they have already become established habits.

Keeping hold of previous Daily Routine versions can be an enlightening thing to do. Looking back on the sheets from 6 months ago, a year ago and even longer can demonstrate just how much progress is being made. This is especially valuable as the process of change and attaining success is mostly a gradual procedure and all too often the changes go unnoticed. Certainly there will be landmark occasions which are notable for the way they dramatically change the direction of life. Creating a written list of goals and producing the first Daily Routine are examples of this kind of sudden progress but much of the journey of success is made up of small steps that are generally overlooked. Being able to look back at some of the activities that were being undertaken in the past can serve to prove just how far the road of success has been travelled. Previous ToDo Lists that have been kept are helpful to refer back to as well as Daily Routines. These should only be used to demonstrate progress; it must always be remembered that the past has gone and the only changes that can be made now are those that are made in the present moment making reference to the future that is desired and defined through written goals.

The Magic of 3 Weeks

Chapter 8

Fitting The Magic into The Day

The process that has been described has largely not taken into account all the daily commitments that everyone already has during their day. For many people this includes a full time job, family responsibilities plus of course the housework that needs to be done regularly. This is before hobbies and leisure activities are added in to the colourful mix that makes up life.

Regardless of how busy life currently is there is always some shuffling around that can be done. What is accomplished in a day are the things that are given highest priority and using the ideas presented in this book, a framework can be created in the form of a Daily Routine that will aid doing the things that will most add to defined goals. Simply completing the tasks of the morning bookend before heading off to work will set one's life on new course more aligned with achieving goals. If time cannot be created before leaving for work then simply have a bookend for lunchtime or even early evening immediately after finishing work. The morning bookend just needs to be completed before the everyday distractions of life get in the away and take up time on things that are not moving life toward long term goals.

If time is really at a premium, start with just a single task in both the morning and the evening bookend. Add three or four tasks for the body of the day and monitor progress after the initial three week period. With a little effort, completing this simple morning bookend will become an ingrained habit and adding another quick task will not seriously impact on the progress of the day. Likewise with the evening bookend, start simple, form the habit and then build up slowly. Each planning weekend will give an opportunity to review what is working and make the changes that are needed moving forwards.

No times of the day are allocated for when specific tasks should be carried out. This means that if something does get in the way it is easy to simply complete the tasks as soon as possible. As always, the morning and evening bookends are the most important tasks to complete and fortunately, these times are also the easiest to control without distraction.

> " Concentrate all your thoughts upon the work at hand. The sun's rays do not burn until brought into focus. "
> **- Alexander Graham Bell**

Having a clear, predefined set of activities to accomplish each day along with a good reason why they are being carried out will make each and every day far more productive. This all starts with dreaming of goals and writing them down and through the process described, arriving at a set of tasks that done consistently, will move you closer to those goals. Keep the end result in mind and the completion of the daily tasks will be less difficult and more rewarding.

Starting with the end in mind creates the focus that will be needed when the task of the Daily Routine seem less than appealing. There will most certainly be times when leaving a task for tomorrow will seem more attractive then starting it today. That choice is certainly yours. However, knowing that a small sacrifice now will bring the goals closer, along with the strange satisfaction of ticking off another completed task, will often provide the necessary motivation to complete just one more task. And it is the extra one completed consistently day after day that can make the all important difference between success and mediocrity in life.

The Magic of 3 Weeks

Chapter 9

Keeping Goals in Focus

A process for dreaming, recording and identifying goals has already been described. We have looked at the way we can recognise which goals are truly important by writing them down from memory so that the ones that persist are the principal goals. We have considered how revisiting them at regular intervals of at least four times each year allows them to evolve as life takes in inevitable twists and turns. Moreover, we have also worked out how to trim the list of goals down and work on just a few at a time to achieve focus.

Even just going through the process as far as identifying and writing down the goals will have a massive effect. Very few people ever get as far as writing down what they want out of their life. Anyone who does is automatically propelled way ahead of the bulk of the population. But like the majority of things, the first part is the most difficult. The good news now is that it does not take much to move even further ahead.

It is possible with very little effort to maintain a greater focus on these goals simply by keeping them in our mind throughout the day. There are numerous techniques for doing this but some of the simplest are also some of the most effective.

Affirmations

The use of affirmations is extremely powerful in all areas of life including goal reinforcement. An affirmation is simply a statement that is repeated regularly so that the subconscious mind believes it to be true and therefore works on creating the beliefs and actions that make it become true.

A successful affirmation needs to be specific and written in the positive, present tense and start with "I have..." or "I am...". To give a couple of examples, these would **not** be good affirmations to use:

> *"I will buy a new car next year"*
> This is not in the present tense and not specific about what type of car.

> *"I have no debts"*
> This is a negative affirmation which will not work. The mind will work on getting debt

> *"I am stopping smoking at New Year"*
> This is neither positive nor present tense.

Instead affirmations need to be specific, positive and present tense. For even more power they should include a deadline. The above affirmations can be rewritten as follows:

> **"I have a black Mercedes sports car by December"**
>
> **"I am debt-free by 28th February"**
>
> **"I am a non-smoker by 1st January"**

In order to be useful, affirmations need to be read out loud at least once per day either immediately after starting the day or last thing at night before sleep. Printing out affirmations and laminating them makes a good bookmark! If reading is something that is done everyday then using the affirmations as a bookmark means that they are always present and can be read out loud at the end of the time spent reading.

Affirmations are not limited to things that we want to have, things that we want to do and changes we want to make. They can be taken further and applied to the mood and outlook we want during the day ahead. Positive affirmations about life and the current day can make an incredible difference when exclaimed out loud at the start of the morning. Here are some examples of these kinds of affirmations that can help change our view of the world around us:

> **"Today is a wonderful day to be alive. Today is the best day and I am going to enjoy every moment of today!"**
>
> **"Ahead of me is a day full of possibilities"**
>
> **"Good morning! Today I will live my life to the full"**
>
> **"Today I will face the world with enthusiasm, energy and joy"**

Morning affirmations about the day ahead can be combined with physical movement first thing in the morning for even greater potency. This could be as simple as a big stretch or they could be incanted with rhythm during a period of exercise.

Many people also choose one or two affirmations and print these out on to paper. The affirmations are then cut out and stuck around the house in conspicuous places such as by the kettle and near the bathroom mirror. An excellent place is on or near to the computer screen as it seems that everyone is forever waiting a short (or perhaps not so short!) time for their computer to do something.

These can then be read out loud during what would otherwise be dead time like waiting for the hot water to make the morning cups of coffee. The same kind of thing can be done with great quotes that are both inspirational and worthy of learning.

Another way to reinforce affirmations is to record them onto CD or as a music file and to play them to yourself often. This can be done while driving, out walking the dog or in the background whilst doing something else. The repetition of hearing them means that they are adopted as fact by the subconscious mind quickly and firmly. The most powerful time to play back a recording of affirmations is during light sleep. They make an ideal way to wake up! Waking up hearing your own affirmations not only imprints them into the mind but also starts the day in a relaxed and positive way which is much better than being woken up by a buzzer or bleeper and definitely more positive than waking up to all the natter and bad news that is found on virtually all radio stations.

> " An affirmation opens the door. It's a beginning point on the path to change."
> **- Louise L. Hay**

Over time the affirmations will become memorised word for word. When this happens they can be used during the course of the day by referring to them whenever you catch yourself thinking or acting against one of your affirmations. Everyone has negative thoughts and doubts themselves from time to time; for some it is more often than for others! As soon as these negative or doubting thoughts are caught they can be counteracted by reciting an appropriate affirmation in one's head or out loud if the situation allows.

" It's the repetition of affirmations that leads to belief. And once that belief becomes a deep conviction, things begin to happen. "

- Claude M. Bristol

Vision Boards

Another effective way to keep focus on the goals that have been set is to have pictures that relate to the completed goals. These can take many forms. One is to produce a collage of pictures with one or more of the images representing a goal. Another way if to have individual pictures pinned up around the house and at work where they will be seen regularly. An especially effective location is the bedroom where they will be seen immediately before going to sleep and first thing after waking up. What better way to start and end the day than with images of the goals that are being worked towards? A further way to display the images is to set them as a screensaver on the computer and/or mobile phone. Of course a combination of these methods can be used and, for many people, using them in combination increases the effectiveness.

> " To visualize is to see what is not there, what is not real - a dream. To visualize is, in fact, to make visual lies. Visual lies, however, have a way of coming true. "
> **- Peter McWilliams**

When choosing images it can quite often be difficult to find something appropriate. If the goal is a new car then the picture is quite easy to choose. It will simply be a picture of the car that is desired which can be found on the internet or cut from a sale brochure. Even better would be a picture of oneself sat in the driving seat of that particular make, model and colour of car. A visit to the showroom should provide the opportunity for getting this.

However, some goals are more difficult to represent in pictures. Learning a foreign language, having dental work carried out and leaving a legacy don't always have appropriate images that spring immediately to mind. A picture of a dentist's chair, a big needle and a drill are probably not the desired images for having dental work completed, it is the result that is the goal and hopefully not the actual process of the work being carried out! In cases like this it is helpful to think about the benefits and lifestyle changes that will be possible once the goal has been achieved. So the goal of having teeth in good order might be to be able to eat food more easily in which case the image of a juicy steak could be appropriate or perhaps it is to have a great smile which can be shown by a picture of oneself with a glistening smile and perhaps a cartoon style bright star. The trick is to be imaginative and to concentrate on the benefit that realising the goal will bring rather than the goal itself.

After a while the images will just blend into the background as they become totally familiar. Therefore it is a good plan to shake them up a bit every now and then. Have fun with moving them around or replacing some or all of them. Fresh pictures can give a fresh perspective on the goals and can often give a fresh drive towards reaching them. Indeed, the very process of finding, selecting and putting up new images will bring those goals to the forefront of the mind which in itself will create energy.

> " Vision without action is merely a dream. Action without vision just passes the time. Vision with action can change the world. "
> **- Joel A. Barker**

Visualisation

Visualising a goal is different from having a vision board with images that represent goals. Visualising involves imagining accomplishing the goal and seeing the images of goal achievement on the screen of the mind. It involves smelling the smells, hearing the sounds and feeling the sensations that will be there when the goal is successfully reached.

Some people find visualisation very easy whereas others need to practice it a great deal before they can use it as an effective technique for moving towards their goals. Either way, it is a skill that is worth the effort it takes to develop as it can be immensely powerful.

When imagining oneself in a scene within the imagination of the mind there are two ways of seeing oneself. A disassociated image is where the person sees their self as a character in the scene and they appear as viewed from outside their own body. Disassociated images can be powerful especially when it comes to visualisation that involves interaction with other people but generally associated images are even more forceful.

In an associated image the person sees the scene through their own eyes; as an actor within the scene. As this is how we all see the real world, this is a very potent form of visualisation.

To use visualisation set aside a time, preferably daily. With closed eyes imagine being in the result of the goal and pay attention to the senses. For example, if the goal is a promotion at work and one of the symbols of that is a prestige office then imagine seeing your name on the wooden door, notice what the name plate is made of, the colour of the writing as you reach for the door handle. Feel the door handle in your hand and notice the shape and texture and open the door. What is the first thing you notice about the office as you step inside? Look at the carpet, smell the wood polish and the leather of the chair. Walk behind the desk and sit down noticing how your body is supported by the chair. Feel the sunlight streaming through the window as you gaze across the desk and picture all the items that are on there, all personal to you especially the photographs.

" Imagination is everything. It is the preview of life's coming attractions. "
- Albert Einstein

When visualising the results of achieving the goal, the more detail and the more of the senses that can be incorporated into the experience, the more effective the result will be. Where possible create memories that will serve as a framework for recreating the scene in the mind. Visiting a car showroom and sitting in your favourite make and model will give the opportunity to grip the steering wheel and notice exactly how it feels while reaching for the gear stick. These memories will then be used as the basis of future visualisation experiences. Even small experiences help greatly so if your goal is to have an office with a leather chair then, next time you sit on a leather sofa pay attention to the feel and the smell so these can be incorporated into your imagined sensations.

Getting used to collecting sensory cues for visualisation experiences has added benefits. It means noticing the world in more detail. The more that is noticed, the more there is to be appreciated and enjoyed. All too often many of the wonderful things that surround each one of us are overlooked due to familiarity. Practising noticing these things in itself can increase the enjoyment of one's life.

Concentrate on goals

It is unfortunate that in our society there appears to exist, a natural preference to think about and to talk about the things that we don't want. It is the things that are thought about and talked about that are given the highest focus. Simply by changing what we choose to think about and talk about we can keep our goals in the forefront of our minds.

Try to catch yourself when you are about to think of the negative side of a situation and instead look for the good. It might start raining and you can think that it is wonderful because it means that garden won't need watering; there really is a positive side to every situation if enough effort is made to look for it. Sometimes finding the good in something can be very difficult but it is always there even if it is well hidden.

Always practice thinking about and talking about your goals and about the good things in your life. Attempt to avoid talking about the difficulties that we all experience in life. Quite quickly you will notice a more generally positive feeling. But also you will start to notice opportunities that will lead closer to achieving your goals. These opportunities were possibly there all the time, but by focussing on what we want by thinking about and talking about our goals, these everyday opportunities come into focus and we are better equipped to see them and take advantage of them.

You may like to challenge yourself talk to someone at least twice every day about your goals by just bringing it into usual conversation. This will have a massive effect on your thinking and also on those around you. Try it for yourself for three weeks and observe the difference for yourself.

> " Whatever we plant in our subconscious mind and nourish with repetition and emotion will one day become reality. "
> **- Earl Nightingale**

The Magic of 3 Weeks

Chapter 10

Is It Worth It?

Is It Worth It?

There is no doubt that allocating time to set some goals takes effort. Then actually setting those goals and making plans for how they can be achieved takes determination. Turning those tasks into a Daily Routine takes concentration and finally sticking to the Daily Routine day after day takes commitment. It is very easy not to do any of the above and that, of course, is your choice.

However, following this simple process doesn't take a great deal of effort, determination or concentration. It is easy to start the process and set the goals, plan the goals and create the Daily Routine. The place where pitfalls linger is in the Daily Routine itself. This takes motivation to follow day after day and inevitably there will be days when we really do not feel like doing any of the tasks on the sheet. This is human nature. The boxes on the sheet are deliberately small so there is no room to write any kind of excuse in there. What matters is whether the task was completed or not. The reason either way is irrelevant. It has to be accepted that the everyday twists and turns of life will sometimes get in the way of the best laid plans. Life has a tendency to throw out unexpected circumstances, both good and bad, at irregular times to keep us alert.

If you have an especially busy day one day then just completing the morning and evening bookends is probably all that is totally necessary and everything in between is a bonus for that day. But these should be exceptional days. If this happens more than about once per week then you have been too ambitious in creating the Daily Routine and, at the next Planning Weekend, it would be advisable to include fewer tasks. Likewise we all have days when we feel more lethargic and less motivated. Again, completing the bookends is the essential activity and everything else is a bonus. When motivation is elusive it can be helpful to first complete the morning bookend then to recognise that any activity means progress. With this in mind, any task that is completed for that day is positive and forgetting about the order of the tasks can work wonders for that day alone. It is important that there is determination to start and next day with more usual vigour.

> " A little more persistence, a little more effort, and what seemed hopeless failure may turn to glorious success. "
> **- Elbert Hubbard**

Is It Worth It?

When times get tough and completing the tasks gets difficult, that is the time to go back to your goals and remind yourself exactly why these boxes are being ticked. It is at such times that the power of a vision board and affirmations come into their own. Keeping pictures in front of you that represent your goals can have a major effect on driving you to do just that little bit more. And that really is the essence of the Daily Routine. It is there to help motivate its user to just do *a little bit more.*

It is by consistently doing a little bit more to move towards achieving the goals that have been set that ultimately results in those goals coming to fruition. If the processes described in this book help us to maintain that consistency and help us to live our dream by achieving our goals, then by that definition at least; yes, it is worth it.

A simple process that repeats every three week that, in each step gets us measurable closer to getting what we really want out of life...that is the Magic of Three Weeks.

> " I don't want to get to the end of my life and find that I just lived the length of it. I want to live the width of it as well. "
> **- Diane Ackerman**

The Magic of 3 Weeks

Epilogue

Epilogue

You have my complete respect and admiration. You have read through this book. That deserves respect in itself.

I was told recently that 87% of non-fiction books are never read. I'm unsure whether to believe this or not as the same person told me that 83.6% of statistics are made up on the spot! But one thing is sure; not many people are prepared to invest the time, money and learning into making their life better.

Whether this is the first book for have read on your journey towards the good life or whether it is just the latest in a long series, you are special because you have now embarked on a striving for self-improvement. Not many people ever take the first step and even fewer keep going. So well done!

You now have a group of ideas that you can use in your own life. You also have a blueprint of the method of using a Daily Routine that I use because it works for me. That is the important part – I use it because it works for me. It is now up to you to try the ideas that appeal to you and find what works. Inevitably some of what suits my personality will not be so applicable to yours.

Take from this book, and from every other book you read just a few ideas and apply them. Combine the ideas from various places into a system that works for you. When you find an idea that you think might work for you, try it and see. Be prepared to try it out, modify and adapt it until you discover a way that it suits you and don't be afraid to drop it if it is not working for you.

If you pick up just two ideas from every book you read then the time you have invested reading has been worthwhile. But once you have the ideas, they need to be applied. They need to be put into action. It is action that propels us along the road towards the good life.

I wish you all the best on your unique journey.

Examples

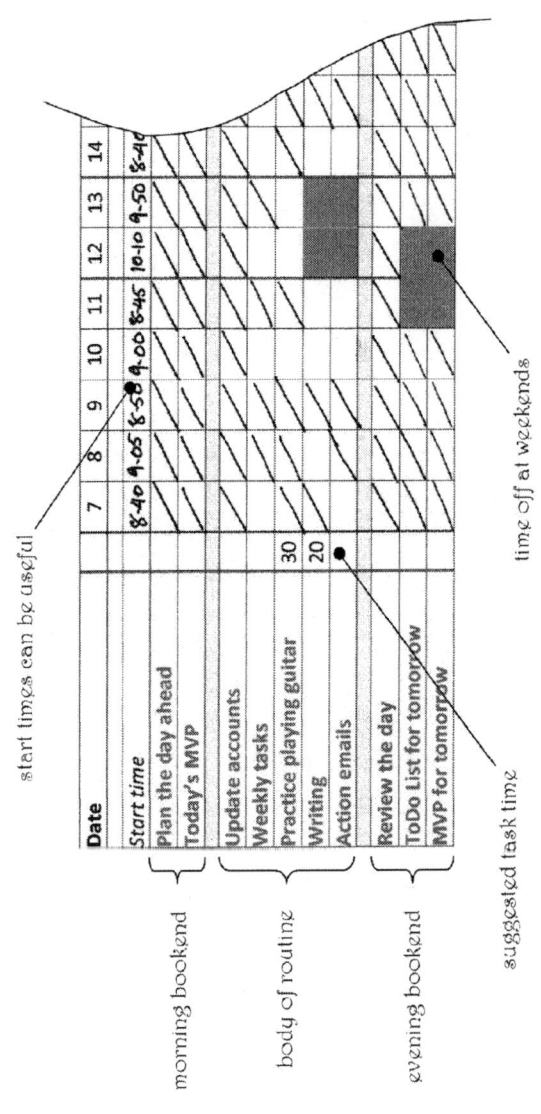

start times can be useful

Date		7	8	9	10	11	12	13	14
Start time		8-40	9-05	8-50	9-00	8-45	10-10	9-50	8-40
Plan the day ahead									
Today's MVP									
Update accounts									
Weekly tasks									
Practice playing guitar	30								
Writing	20								
Action emails									
Review the day									
ToDo list for tomorrow									
MVP for tomorrow									

morning bookend

body of routine

evening bookend

suggested task time

time off at weekends

86